ONE HUNDRED YEARS

One Hundred Years
First Edition

First published in the United Kingdom in 2021 by Hoxton Mini Press
Copyright © Hoxton Mini Press 2021. All rights reserved.

All photographs © Jenny Lewis
Introduction by Lucy Davies
Sequence by Jenny Lewis and Hoxton Mini Press
Copy-editing by Florence Filose
Design by Daniele Roa
Production by Anna De Pascale

A CIP catalogue record for this book is available from the British Library.

ISBN 978-1-910566-85-5

Hoxton Mini Press would like to thank those that invested in our future:
Andrew, Laura and Raphael Beaumont, Anonymous, David Rix, Don McConnell,
Duncan, Liss and Theo, Fiona and Gordon (Bow), Gareth Tennant, Gary,
Graham McClelland, Herlinde, Jenifer Roberts, Jennifer Barnaby, Joe Skade,
Jonathan Crown, Jonathan J. N. Taylor, Matt Jackson, Melissa O'Shaughnessy,
Nigel S, Rob Phillips, Rory Cooper, Simon Robinson and Steev A. Toth.

This book is 100% carbon compensated according to ClimateCalc (climatecalc.eu).
Offset purchased from: Stand For Trees.

Printed and bound by: Livonia, Latvia

To order books, collector's editions and signed prints please go to:
www.hoxtonminipress.com

ONE HUNDRED YEARS

Portraits of a community aged 0–100

Photography and interviews by

Jenny Lewis

HOXTON MINI PRESS

Books in the series:

To order books, collector's editions and signed prints go to:
www.hoxtonminipress.com

East London Photo Stories

Book Sixteen

To Duncan, who has shared

26 years of my journey.

INTRODUCTION

This strange, beautiful, treacherous life. What does it mean?
So many pen nibs and paint brushes and cans of film have been
expended over the years in contemplation of that question,
and we are only marginally the wiser.

The hitch has been that life is generally – wildly, gloriously –
ungraspable when you're in the middle of it. And stepping outside
is impossible. Consequently, only the parts you have already
played, or, less clearly, are presently playing, become visible. Never
the parts to come. Never the whole.

Look backwards and there behind you, shifting and settling
in your wake, is a sort of dot-to-dot composed of choices made and
paths taken that add up to where you are now. Hindsight smooths
any anomalies, of course. We prefer a pattern – our brains love
them – because patterns suggest meaning.

Try to apply the same to the now, though, or to what might be in
your cards, and it gets messier. All those possible outcomes make for
the kind of unruly snarl you see if you turn a piece of embroidery
over. The loose threads. The stops and starts. The part-stitched hopes.

I think this is at least part of what makes *One Hundred Years* so
riveting. Its reach and flow administer a sense of life that is far
deeper and richer than could ever be expressed by a single picture.

It's life as only a god might see it: from first to last, incrementally
unfolding, like the leathery yawn of an accordion bellows, or
one of those time-lapse films that capture the slow rampage of
an Alaskan glacier.

Of course, domestic, unheroic life such as is pictured here, with its problems and compromises and its great sloshes and streaks of unutterable joy, is tiny in comparison to an eons-old ice field. But it can also be everything, especially to the one living it, or to those whose lives it touches.

Perhaps you think you have a typical, ordinary life. Most of us do. But read even a tenth of the 100 stories that are chattering and rustling away inside here, and you will grasp that there is no such thing. It's shocking, actually, to scratch at the surface and see the gorgeously rich earth.

I wonder, too, if some of the things that are voiced in these pages have been spoken about in years – if at all. I suppose we're not often encouraged to talk about ourselves, to tell our own tale, so when that chance does come, it pours out. The stories near drench you.

Here are some of the things I have learnt from them: that the slow accretion of lived days can scrape away self-knowledge as well as bestow it. That people can change, though not all of them will, or want to. That old ladies will always be the first to get up and dance. How much I miss the blind confidence of youth.

That I could be capable of anything under certain circumstances. That what we want rarely matches up with what we get (though what we get is usually better for us). That we will almost certainly disappoint a few people along the way, but we will also bring great comfort. That humour is everything.

Curiously, the one thing that resists comprehension here is ageing. The only rule about ageing, it seems, is that there are no rules about ageing. Just look at the number of brisk, bright faces in their eighties and nineties, or at the wise, knowing ones in the early pages of the book. As for things like contentment and loss, pain and growth – well, they come and go as they please.

Perhaps it is the opposition between the tremendous scope of this project, and the close-up idiosyncrasies of the lives it contains, which makes it so potent. 100 fragments, cut from their context. The first lines of 100 stories. But oh, what stories. To look into their eyes, and to hear all that they have chosen to share, is to feel let in on the best kind of secret.

Lucy Davies, 2021

Nellie, 105 years old

A NOTE FROM THE PHOTOGRAPHER

I've thought for a while now, that the ordinary is actually pretty extraordinary. You don't have to look far to find the good stuff on your doorstep.

It happens. We are drawn to our own tribe – people with a similar path, the same fears, people at the same stage of life that we can relate to. But isn't it more interesting to stop and lift your gaze from your own life and observe what else is going on? To really listen to the experience of our elders, or reflect on a more youthful, uncluttered view?

I met Nellie when she was 105, and took her portrait for Mother's Day back in 2018. I couldn't have been more engaged by her company, hungrily gathering up the snippets of her life. We didn't spend long together, as she was dressed and ready to go to church. My time was up, but her energy and attitude got me thinking: how could I engineer this kind of life lecture?

Over the last three years, I have used photography to invite myself into 100 different shoes in my community, capturing people of every age from birth to 100. I've visited social clubs and parks, tennis courts and allotments, homes and workplaces, encouraging participants to nominate others that have touched their lives.

My perception of what I thought I knew was continually tested. These were meaningful conversations, with depth and vulnerability, encompassing all human emotion and experience. Lives that ebb and flow, changing course at any moment. I was given insight into the fragility of it all, and the human capacity for resilience.

Recently, I was struck by the words of poet Amanda Gorman, as she recited at the Capitol: 'As we grieved, we grew.' It's clear to me now, from the many people I've met while making *One Hundred Years*, that every sorrow we endure helps us live a little deeper, love a little stronger, experience the world with a few more hues.

Human interaction has an energy. It recharges the batteries in a way nothing else can. Working on this series has changed how I want to engage with the world, and the people in it. My hope is that it might cause a shift in your perspective, might encourage you to lift your gaze, too.

Thank you to all the people who agreed to participate in this project, the 100 in this book and the many others gathered along the way.

Jenny Lewis, 2021

'What is the meaning of life? That was all – a simple question; one that tended to close in on one with years. The great revelation had never come. The great revelation perhaps never did come. Instead there were little daily miracles, illuminations, matches struck unexpectedly in the dark.'

Virginia Woolf, *To the Lighthouse*

HERB

0 years old

AROKO

1 year old

'Daddy.'

RORY

2 years old

'Have it, eat it, apple.'

VIVI

3 years old

'My favourite food is alien food. I like to be loud every day.'

JOY

4 years old

'Red. Green. Orange. Purple. Yellow. White.
These are my favourite colours.'

RAY

5 years old

'If I made a magic potion it would turn someone small so they can fit under the sofa.'

'How long would they be under the sofa for?'

'For one year.'

ROMEO

6 years old

'I already know what I'm going to do. But
I don't want to do it, because I need lots
of money to do it. And I dunno how to get
that money.

I'd like to be a rock star.'

JACK

7 years old

'People are always stereotypical to me.
Just because I'm a boy they say you can't like
pink, but I love pink. One of the first times
I wore a skirt, my mum bought me a tutu.
I looked in the mirror and I loved it. It makes
me feel happy when I'm glamorous.'

BLANCHE

8 years old

'I have a black eye because I was playing sword fighting with a cardboard tube. It's my fourth black eye.

The only thing that would scare me is if a sabre-toothed tiger came up to me.

I do get worried sometimes. I get loads of thoughts, at night-time mostly. When one comes, then another one comes, then another one comes. I write things that worry me down. It doesn't look as scary then.'

CASSIUS

9 years old

'I'd like to be described as a person who does
what he wants to. A free person.'

TEYA

10 years old

'No one at my new school made me feel weird
about having two mums. I said it to loads
of people to see how people would react and
mostly everyone has been nice about it so
it's not something I worry about.'

HERB

11 years old

'Whatever I do I have to do it 100%. I'm not
interested in the middle. I used to have long,
blond hair to my shoulders and then I decided
I wanted it all off. Like when I went vegetarian
one day overnight, no sweets with gelatine,
completely vegetarian and then I just went back
three years later completely not vegetarian.
Now I just love meat.'

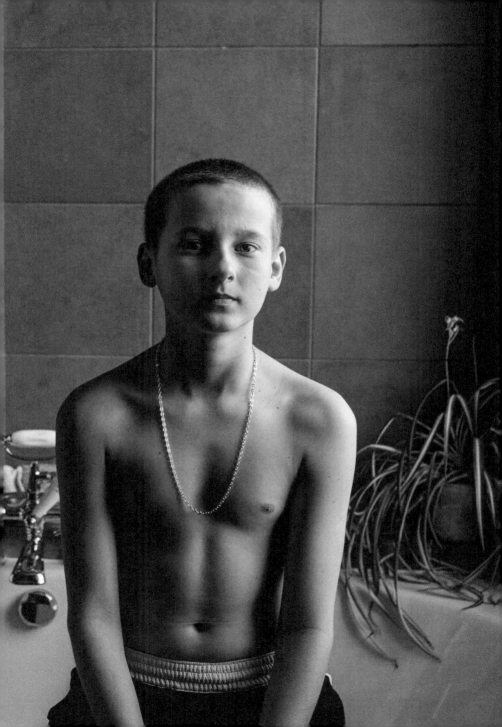

THEIA

12 years old

'A teacher said, "Young man at the back, what's your name?" So I said, "I'm a girl." She said, "Hi Miguel," and I was like, "No, I'm a girl." I said that, like, two more times and then my friend just said, "She's a girl," and the teacher said, all flustered, "Oh, I'm sorry, I didn't have my glasses on."

I just got World No. 2 for my age in BMX. I'm definitely thinking Olympics. It feels like it's in reach.'

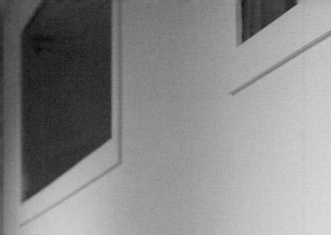

RUBY

13 years old

'Teenagers are annoying and even I find
myself annoying.

Sometimes I talk back a bit because I have
a voice and I have an opinion and I can
express it.'

ARRAN

14 years old

'I don't feel the same excitement I did as a child,
nothing seems to feel like the explosive joy you used
to get on Christmas Day.

I'm happiest when hanging out with my best mate,
Stanley. I don't even really think of him as a friend.
I think the phrase "brother from another mother" is a
good fit. I think life has a weight. The more you've been
through, the harder it gets to carry alone and when
you have someone that knows you as well as me and
Stanley know each other, you can share that weight.

But Batman is still my first love, you just can't beat
Batman.'

NIA

15 years old

'I push myself and I push myself, like I do with everything.
I don't like losing. I always want to be first and be at
the front. I'm always going to try my hardest to win.
That's my motto, I just want to win.

I did one of my raps about racism in front of the whole
school. If I was rubbish at rapping it would be different,
but I know I'm good.'

MIA

16 years old

'I moved into this studio in the garden when I turned 16 and we've agreed that I can live here until I move out.

My desire to leave home was so strong, but impractical at my age, so this was the compromise we reached. Now I have this sanctuary.'

ETHAN

17 years old

'I'm not sure I've got over my last relationship, which is
probably pretty dumb, I should probably hop to it.
I feel like now I want to not hunt for people but instead
improve myself and let people come to me, using
my own talent. I mean, I'm just a chill guy chilling in
the park so maybe someone will eventually see that.
It's kind of, like, a philosophy.'

CHARDE

18 years old

'When I left care I was referred for acting workshops.
I was so shy, I couldn't instigate conversation.

In the theatre group, they gave me a character that was
a complete contrast to my personality. It was really
hard and uncomfortable to be this confident character,
but by playing that role it gave me a way to come out of
my shell. It's a valuable tool: fake it till you make it.'

SAMARI

19 years old

'I've always been round big people and that's where
I gather my information. I can ask them something and
they can give me a better acknowledgement, instead
of asking someone my age. I rather ask someone that
been through it, gone through it already and have
the experience. I feel my mind is a bit older than people
my own age.'

IRIS

20 years old

'I'm living at home with my mum and my little brother
and I love it. I absolutely love it, even though I'm getting
to that age when I should move out.

Mum is thinking of moving back to Brazil for good so
I'm probably going to end up here alone, which is
just way worse than me moving out as she's going to
be so far away.

I wish I was younger to be honest, so I didn't have
to rush to move out and do certain things.'

TARIK

21 years old

'When my mum and dad split up, I was 11 and starting
secondary school. I wanted to make some quick
money and I was gullible, so I got into the gangs. They
treated me like a family, like a brother – that's where
they are clever – but at that age you don't know that.
Now I understand.

My brother got stabbed and one of his friends died.
The guy came from nowhere, just out the front of
our house he stabbed my brother and my dad and he
tried to stab me in the back. My mum watched it all.
The worst thing is I knew his nan, his mum, everything,
but he was in the other gang.

I wasn't innocent.

I don't carry knives or nothing now. I had to move,
disappear. I couldn't leave my house for fear of getting
jumped. I'm glad I moved. My brother is totally out
of it now, at university. I'm getting my mum out of here.
I'm trying to become a pilot. I just got to get my GCSEs.
I want to study, I love science, physics. I'm ready for
the world.'

RAMZIA

22 years old

'Falling in love definitely makes your
priorities shift.'

ALEX

23 years old

'When you've been told at a young age that you mean
nothing, you don't matter, you're not focused, then you
act like it.

Now I work with kids. I'm very careful not to use
any harsh or negative adjectives towards them, because
it sticks, and I would rather help them find who they
really are than plant a negative seed in their brain.'

AMARA

24 years old

'My mum never knew how she was going to make ends meet, but I never felt like I had to want or need for anything. She always calls me and my sister her projects, her greatest achievements. I just think she's the strongest woman I've ever met.

I'm so happy with where I am right now. I have a great job, it's creative, it pays well, everyone is friendly. My biggest thing is financial stability; I never want to feel I have to rely on anyone else to provide for me. I'm constantly working to retain my independence.'

JOSH

25 years old

'I talk very slowly. I go over everything I'm going to
say in my head, like a script, checking it's safe.
I've always thought that's just the way I am, but recently
I discovered it's a common trait among survivors of
childhood abuse.

Everyone is shaped by their experiences, whether it's
trauma or privilege. We all have a choice about how
we respond to whatever happened to us.'

Leo

26 years old

'I moved here from Australia when I was 18, knowing
no one. The thought of doing something like that
now is absolutely terrifying.

I never really experienced anxiety until I was 24.
I was so confident, then suddenly I'm like this anxious
mess, and now I'm, like, freaking out. It's weird.
I think maybe it's a lot to do with fear of the future.
It's a big shift in energy or something.'

EDWIN

27 years old

'I spent most of my childhood wanting to be an adult and I'm thrilled to be here. Can't complain.

You think you go to school to learn everything then get on with your life, but the rest of your life is spent learning the things they didn't teach you in school.'

HATTIE

28 years old

'I don't take myself seriously but I take my work very seriously. My work gives me a sense of calm, it gives me structure. It sounds dramatic but I need this focus beyond myself. It is, of course, obsessive.'

K*ENDALL ON CARA

justin

The best is yet to come

ARTIST

HANDS OFF

SPECIAL F

WARHOL

ARTIST ROOMS

SUSANA

29 years old

'I look at other people and friends and they're
getting married and having kids. I don't want to get
married, that's not the thing at all, but they just
seem to have an established life, and I'm just like,
"Oh shit!"'

Sam

30 years old

'My generation is probably the last that grew up
without social media and I think we were very lucky
to just be ourselves. I understand the compulsion,
but it's just not for me. I don't have social media or
seek that trigger. I'd like to think I don't seek other
people's approval, which is not to say I don't want to
be liked, but I have no interest in taking pictures
of myself having a good time.'

ARCHIE

31 years old

'My dad had a cancer diagnosis that gave him less than a year.

I've lost the person I was always most excited to share stuff with. He was good at having a light touch, he backed me and my sibling with complete faith. To have someone you completely trust and respect believe in you is such great fuel. That confidence is now in me, even though he's not here.'

SONIA

32 years old

'I'm more ready for motherhood now than when
I was 21. I have more experience, I have learnt lessons,
what I can do better. I think I was really young when
I had my first child. I knew nothing. I did not know
what sort of a mother I would be.'

PUYA

33 years old

'My sister's son, Darian, is 4 and has a condition called GM1 gangliosidosis. Watching the person you love most in the world slowly die burns away a lot of the bullshit.

Fuck, I love that kid. He's taught me more in his four short years on this planet than I've learnt in my three decades on it. He's taught me what unconditional love really looks like. Acceptance for things I cannot change. A sense of living in the present because you truly don't know how much longer any of us have in this world, and to make each and every moment as joyful as possible.

He's given me a resilience I never knew possible. I can experience such immense pain but still find joy in life, because I've learnt to process an unfathomable thing.'

MARTHA

34 years old

'This stage of life has surprised me. I thought I'd be the perfect mum. I thought I could give and give and give. But then I turned around and realised I was totally depleted. You think you're throwing love at someone, behaving with the best intentions, but what your children actually need is to see you taking care of yourself; saying no sometimes. I can tell them whatever I tell them, but what they're going to learn is what they see me doing.'

MARK

35 years old

'I was very insecure about the way I looked, being poor, growing up not having the same things as everyone else. I acted confident but I wasn't confident inside.

I became more confident in my twenties, when I realised those things aren't so important. Just be you.'

ROSY

36 years old

'A cancer diagnosis is devastating at any time, but felt especially cruel during pregnancy. I felt all my joy being stolen. Slowly, since the moment he was pulled from my belly, Herb has given it back to me day by day. Building me up, returning me to the person I was.

It's been the worst year and the best year of my life. I've experienced complete extremes: deep sorrow and unimaginable happiness.

When you're thinking about dying every day, looking after a new life is perhaps the best remedy of all.'

JOHN

37 years old

'I always remember Grayson Perry saying that being an artist is a middle-class job – running your own business. He explained it in such an ordinary way. I don't want to be middle class, but hearing it explained like that helped make being an artist just a normal occupation.

I feel happier in my thirties, but also really just at the start of my career. I take a lot of comfort when I see people that I really admire in their fifties and sixties who are just getting recognition. I don't want to hurry. I don't want anything other than to keep going, working with nice people and making a living.'

KING

38 years old

'I was arrested for doing a graffiti mission the day
before my wedding – I made it out a few hours before
the ceremony – but when my first child was born, that
was it. I promised my wife I was done.

There are four kids now looking up to me. It's what
I signed up for. They need me and I'm hungry for it.
Can you imagine the amount of times I hear "Daddy"
each day?

This is my life and I love it.'

Hatt

39 years old

'Boats are real time as opposed to virtual time.
I can get the internet on the boat, but there's always
so much to do. That physical activity, being outside
in the rain and the snow and the sun, draws you
into the real world.

My daughter loves the boat. She knows the
difference between a swan and a cormorant and
a hen, and she's only 3.'

RICH

40 years old

'Being a bus driver teaches you to be calm and be humble. You're observing all day long. You're often invisible.

You might see a person one day and they'll be really rude, then another day they'll be polite. It depends how their day's going. It makes you think about different people's lives, and the stresses they might be going through.

I've been doing it 14 years now. You learn a lot.'

NATALIE

41 years old

'I've been taught to think that there's an element of
selfishness to keep pursuing whatever pleases me.
But I've had to resist living the way other people would
prefer me to live. I'm very lucky that I've always done
what I wanted to do. I'm not afraid of change – in fact
change is a motivator for me. I like putting myself
in uncomfortable situations.'

ANKA

42 years old

'I had anorexia, bulimia and everything in between.
To me, it felt like an addiction, like being an alcoholic.
It's a distraction from life.

I don't see my traumas as doom and gloom, but as
positive things – they are my chapters, you know?
My family is my close group of friends, and my partner.
We're solid: both very independent, free souls, but
together. I always call it "together alone" – and that's
where I'm most comfortable.'

SHANAZ

43 years old

'I never smile. If you smile, you might get a beating.
If you laugh, you're too happy, you're going to
get a beating. If you haven't had a beating for a few
days, you start to feel anxious that there'll be another
one soon, that he's just building up to it. He used to
work away at a restaurant three nights a week,
and I think that's how I survived for so long. I knew
I had three clear days a week.

Now I go where I want, I wear what I want, I say
what I want, I do what I want, I eat what I want.
I've got freedom.

My toaster was broken and my dad asked my brother
to get me a new one. I was livid when it turned up.
I don't want anyone choosing a toaster for me, I'll choose
my own. Everything in this house is mine. I bought it
with my own money. I had all the choices taken away
from me for so long that having choice is a pleasure,
there's joy in it. It's not a fantastic toaster but that's not
the point. It's mine and I chose it.'

FABIEN

44 years old

'The most important thing for me about teaching tennis
is that I love working with children. Children are
funny. I was teaching this little boy, having a rally, we're
both enjoying it, and then he accidentally called me
"Dad". He put his hand over his mouth, it was really
sweet and he was embarrassed. I said, "Bless you."'

Vivan

45 years old

'As I get older, I think that I should consider settling
down somewhere, but then I realise that as long as
I have the means to travel, and to visit family and friends
for extended times, then I can call anywhere home.'

ALGY

46 years old

'In today's world we are always so fucking busy and
then we fill it with another project, a side hustle.
Should we not just fill it with daydreaming, or playing
with the kids a bit more? We can hide behind work,
it's hard to just *be*.'

LESLEY

47 years old

'I love getting older. I love it.

The key thing in the last few years is that my irresponsibility has come back. My motto this year, my New Year's resolution, is "Be more disappointing to people." It's great, it's so liberating to not have to get it right all the time.

I try and meet men my own age, but it's just, it's hard when there's a buffet of readily available, fun younger men. They have less baggage but they come with other issues: they love to talk about their feelings.

And then the other thing is the porn. They're all growing up with immediate access to porn so their first sexual experiences are porn whereas our first sexual experiences were sexual experiences. They watch porn and then they apply it. You're in their porno, often as the older woman. I'm perfectly entertained, but after a number of them I think they've probably all watched the same film.'

Emma

48 years old

'I really wanted my mum to be alive, I loved her and
she was brilliant – properly an amazing mum – but she
hated being ill. She had a neurodegenerative disease.
When she said she wanted to go to Dignitas, we said,
"That's a shit idea, we love you and we want you to
stay here with us."

It took a year for us to come round. She didn't
persuade us, she just kept saying, "I know this is hard."
She contained us through this terrible time, it was
a brilliant bit of mothering.'

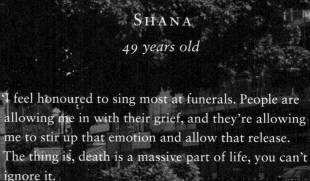

SHANA

49 years old

'I feel honoured to sing most at funerals. People are allowing me in with their grief, and they're allowing me to stir up that emotion and allow that release. The thing is, death is a massive part of life, you can't ignore it.

I've had five brain surgeries. I chose to do life. For my children, for me, for people around me, I chose to do life. I have found that by doing so, life is great.'

WILFRID

50 years old

'I feel a little bit sheepishly luxurious in my life,
compared to people who have to go to work
every day and do what they don't want to do.'

SEAN

51 years old

'I went to drama school when I was 41. Everyone else
was in their twenties. I found out that acting was
a lot harder than I imagined. It's been a rollercoaster
ride: weeks, months where there's lots of money
and then months when there isn't. Where's the next
job coming from? Now, every day is different. I can't
really express myself unless I'm acting.'

Angus

52 years old

'All gardening – but particularly vegetable gardening –
is brutal. All that work and then it's gone. Like a
profound antidote to consumerism, you can't possess
a garden.

I love the contrast of the city and the sound of the sirens,
cars, trains. There's a real soundscape. The allotment
has become my palette. I'm continuously building
different compositions.'

EMMA

53 years old

'My dad always said you should help someone
over 80 once a week, at least once a week.
My dad always said that, and that's why I think
I'm in these jobs. Caring. I love it. I love caring
for people.'

Nhi

54 years old

'The greatest challenge of my life is that my husband
has leukaemia. Derek is a purist: he doesn't take
Western drugs, he doesn't want to take Chinese
medicine, for him healing is natural. He won't accept
any help.

I'm a healer and I can't heal him. We couldn't be more
yin and yang. I'm trying to figure out what is this lesson
that life is trying to teach me – is it that you can't
change people? We need to be constantly taught that
we can't change the world.'

ANJUM

55 years old

'Everybody has the right to be their true and best self,
so coming out, as a Muslim and a lesbian and a mum –
being open, being true, not hiding – is the best thing
I have ever done.

I love being in my fifties. I really had no idea of the
consolidation, the courage, the comfort, the child,
this decade would bring out in me, but here I am, full
of life and joy. More free-spirited than ever.'

LEN

56 years old

'At 18, it was key for me to have someone older in my
life to guide me. I was so happy and proud to work
for Joe. Everyone just loved the man. We could trust each
other, he was 100% my mentor. We worked together
for 25 years until he got really sick from cancer.
He deteriorated so quickly.

I bought the workshop and changed everything over to
my name. He was more a father to me than my actual
father, the connection was very powerful.

Knowing how important it is to have a mentor I've
carried on that tradition. You can see the effect on kids
when their father isn't there that much. You have to
listen so they can talk. You hold their hand until they
let go and then you see them fly.'

SASKIA

57 years old

'The older I've got, the more I enjoy acting.
I thought that after I'd had my family I might
have softened and let go a bit, but actually
I'm more fiercely passionate.'

Bo

58 years old

'The minute you become a father, you have such
a strong link to your child. It changed my whole life.
It was seismic.

But now, having a 14 year old, I sharply feel a silence.
She's moving on and I'm not. It's a grieving process,
a surprising loss – not a death, but a shift in the
relationship.'

ROB

59 years old

'You need an incredible doggedness to be an artist.
I was always fairly positive that I'd make my living out
of my art, but it took a while to happen – it wasn't till
I was about 40 that it kicked off. Even when I started to
have success my dad was still saying, "Why don't
you become a picture framer on the side to make a
bit of cash?"

There's a part of me that wants to keep going and create
more and more, but there's also a side that thinks
maybe I can relax a bit now, and not be pushing myself
so hard all the time. Having said that, there are still
stories I want to tell, there are still things I want to do.'

CYNTHIA

60 years old

'I liken the menopause to being an adolescent, but
the other way around. Your head, your expectations,
it all starts shifting. Your body starts controlling you.
As far as men are concerned, you are going mad,
but that's not it. It's the second time you discover
yourself. It's beautiful, you know? It's life.'

ANOOP

61 years old

'She was 20 and I was 24 when we were introduced by family. We got married after nine days and after six months we went into business together. We've always been partners in everything. We still enjoy each other's company like we did when we were young.'

KIMBERLEY

62 years old

'A friend of mine brought their niece and nephew
round. He was like, "I told them we were going to a
museum." I didn't know if it was a compliment or
not. They couldn't stop talking about it to their parents.
"Do we pay you?" They really thought it was a sort of
gallery that I only opened to special people, you know.

He brought her back a while ago as she'd asked to
come back to the museum. It's quite sweet.'

GEOFF

63 years old

'My parents were really strict, and yet they let me
have 14 arcade machines in my tiny bedroom. I was
a pinball hustler. First time I played, it was literally love
at first sight. It was like a religion to me. The machines
seemed alive, with personalities. I'd practise for eight
hours a day. My parents were a little worried about me.
I've got about 190 pinball machines now. I chat to
them in my workshop.'

ROMILLY

64 years old

'I have created a house and a garden that I love.
I have survived my predicament, 15 years of multiple
scleroris, because of my creativity. Without that it
would have been very hard. I sometimes find a
microcosm of the world in very small places, perhaps
a miniature landscape of moss. There is beauty and
drama if you just take time to look.

Compared to a lot of people in my situation I'm very
fortunate. I'm a pretty optimistic and happy person.
I don't want to live my life feeling miserable.'

FERNANDO

65 years old

'British seriousness makes me feel uncomfortable
sometimes. In Latin culture it is normal to
touch other people, embrace and show warmth.
Human contact is very important for me.'

JILL

66 years old

'We've travelled more in the last six years than I ever had, because my partner's eyesight is failing and we want to see as much as we can together before it goes. It's been the best time of my life.'

NICK

67 years old

'The nice thing about being 67 is that you don't have that monkey on your back: you've done your career. What you do now is just magic.'

ERIC

68 years old

'I don't see that I'm in the process of living, I see
myself as in the process of dying. I don't see this as
a negative thing, I see it as a positive. Death is a friend.
It's a journey and you're coming to some station
point. It's not something to be frightened of, or walk
away from, ignore or deny. Death is a healthy
process of life.'

Elaine

69 years old

'I've never lived on my own. I'm finding it fun.
The only time I find it really scary is alone in bed at
night. That accentuates the fact that there is no
partner in my life anymore. And I'm beginning to
realise that might be permanent. That's the biggest
sadness, but there's fuck all I can do about it.

I miss sex. Christ yes! And that to me is bizarre,
because for me a whole life includes that. And yet
somehow I can't have it, I'm not allowed it.

It's horrible not being fancied. And I know that is
such an unfeminist thing to say. But I would really
like to be fancied.'

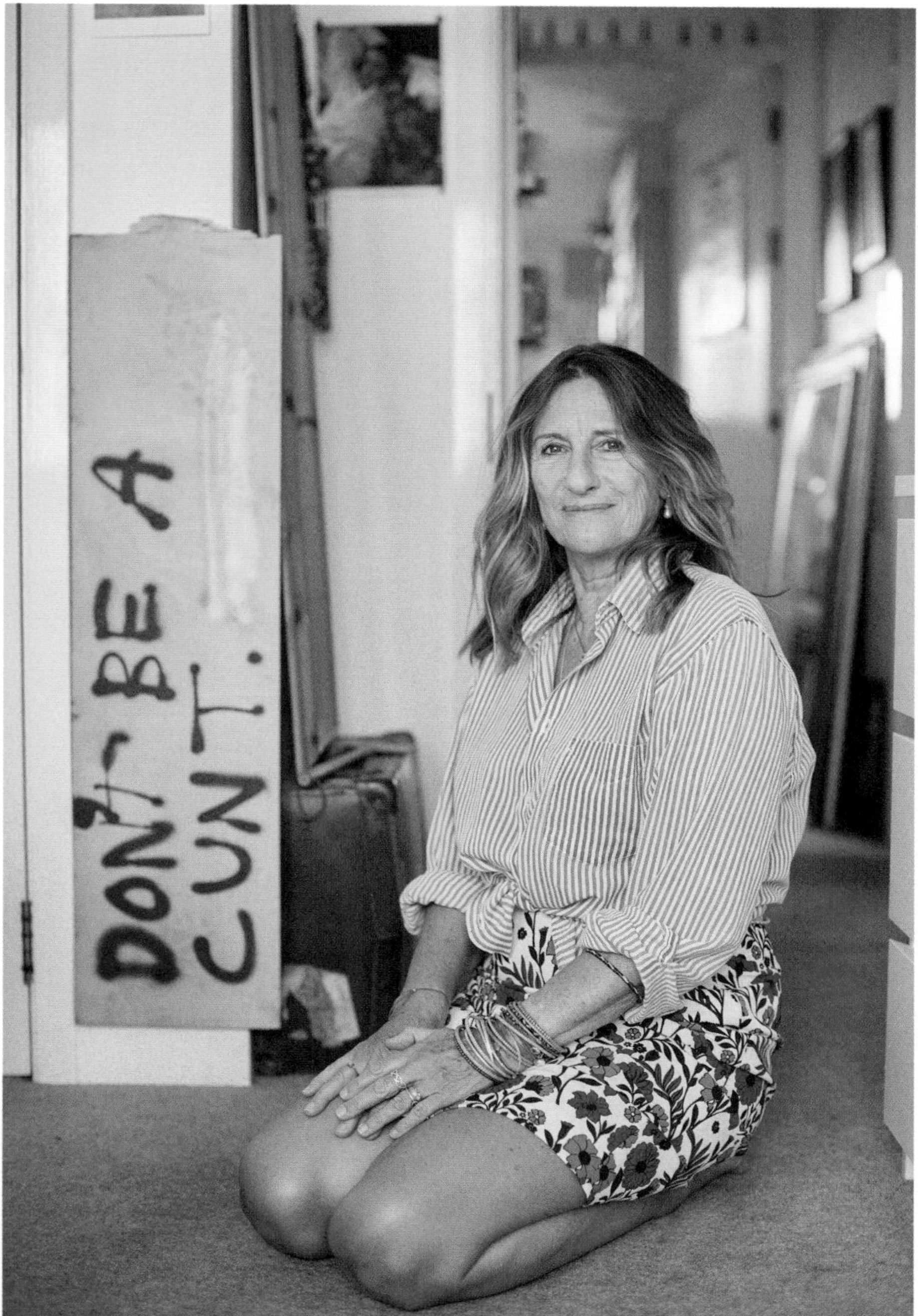
DON'T BE A
CUNT.

HUGH

70 years old

'I'm a failed rock and roll star.

I'm too old now. My harmonica player has just had
a liver transplant; someone else has arthritis and has to
have three days off after playing. Our band is actually
called the Walking Wounded.

We've grown into our name.'

JENNY

71 years old

'Not many people still live in a house share in their
seventies. I don't have many possessions, I've always
been quite transient – living in hotel rooms around
the world for long stretches. I've never wanted my own
front door, being on my own is my idea of hell. My
flatmates are in their thirties. I love being with younger
people and looking at the world in a fresher way,
and of course it's brilliant for help with technology.'

RICK

72 years old

'I was street homeless for 15 years, from my late teens
to early thirties. Extremely cut off. You're just fending
for yourself.

I decided to get an education, so I filled my life with
learning and astonished myself. I started reading books
about science and biology out the library. I signed up
to the Open University, and then a degree, and then
a Master's in biological computation. I was homeless
through the whole thing. When you've done that,
you find that you can be valuable.

Because my life has been so precarious and different,
I just can't quite fit into people's expectations. There's
a sense of disquiet in my life that I can't remove.'

JOAN

73 years old

'My mother had a hard life as a single parent. Being
the only girl, she tried to protect me, and as a teenager
I felt like an egg in a glass case. When I had to tell her
I was going to England to study, she was very sad
and broken-hearted.

I arrived in Peterborough and what do you think I see?
Something that makes my eyes pop: a couple kissing
on the platform. I couldn't believe it, and no one was
batting an eyelid. It was ten in the morning!
Yes, I thought, things are going to be different here.'

PHILIP

74 years old

'The look of success changes as you get
older... It's that old cliché: what matters are
the simple things money can't buy.'

DANI

75 years old

'I was offered elocution once. They might as well have been offering me some pet mice. I was like, no thanks. I'm alright as I am. I don't need to hide my roots.

I was brought up to believe you can make things better. I was surrounded by pretty rough kids on a council estate, but my dad was a professional musician so I had quite a mixed view.

We can't all be lawyers. And you know what, we do need road sweepers, and the ones I speak to are very happy doing it, thank you very much.'

Cloud

76 years old

'In the late 1980s, I was diagnosed HIV positive.
I decided to start a theatre company comprised entirely
of others with the condition. We became a great success.
I witnessed the transformation of frightened individuals,
some terrorised by public ignorance, into confident
performers. It's encouraged me to help others not give
up hope.'

MARGARET

77 years old

'I lived at the Tower of London from 5 to 11.
My brother and I had the most fantastic
childhood there. The moat was our playground,
we played hide and seek in the White Tower.'

JOHN

78 years old

'You know what you want to do, but your body just can't do it anymore. I misjudged that step one time and a tray of vol-au-vents went flying. I had to pick them all up and put them back on the tray. They got eaten, no one noticed. Never trust a buffet.'

DAVID

79 years old

'I got a job as a swimming pool attendant. It was
absolutely the most boring job I'd ever done. It was
horrible, all the small talk, oh it was terrible.
I saw a notice about a driver for the library. I got it
and worked there 27 years.

I'm not very good with small talk. My wife was
wonderful at that. Right away she could hit it off
with anyone. After she died you have to adapt
to the quiet, but it's not been too difficult for me,
I don't really need conversation round me.'

SHERLOCK

80 years old

'I always wore my own clothes that I made. When I arrived here in my twenties, I had a jacket like Liberace with black and silver thread in it. I had a checked shirt, black trousers with white stitching down the sides, moccasins that were off-white, and lime green socks. One said "rock", one said "roll".

When I see my boys in football shirts and tracksuit bottoms made of the nastiest fabric, I think to myself, they should be arrested walking around in those clothes. I wear better things to clean my car… when I had a car.'

GRENVILLE

81 years old

'I've had a pretty vibrant life. I've partied
a lot and misbehaved a bit. At 81, I'm
beginning to learn to be unselfish. It takes
a bit of time, doesn't it?'

ANDREAS

82 years old

'I sleep about three hours a night. I listen to the Greek
radio. After midnight, it's the Cyprus radio. I like
people phoning in and dedicating songs. I miss my old
friends from Cyprus who, one by one, are dying.
I sing in a Greek choir, I keep the language and the
music with me.'

JOHN

83 years old

'Before the war, virtually every garden had pigeons.
People didn't have radios – they didn't have much at
all – so many men, young and old, kept pigeons.
They may also have used them for eating purposes.
Even today, someone will stop and say to me,
"Are you selling them? Can I eat them?"

I still race them but, like me, they're too old really.
I've raced three times this year, but they came last each
time. That's never worried me. I've had some good
times with them.'

LIEN

84 years old

'We came here in 1980, when I was 45.

When I was in Vietnam, life was really tough – maybe
that's why I am still strong now. I worked 16 hours
a day since I was 9 years old, when my mother died.
I was sent away to work for relatives so there was one
less mouth to feed at home.

I had six children of my own, three girls and three boys.
I didn't have any help. I would go to work from 6 a.m.
to midnight, then come home and feed the kids. The
older ones would help with the little ones. My husband
was a lorry driver, so was away a lot of the time.
Everyone around me was going through the same thing.

Now they are all grown up, they make their own
money. I save and give some back to the elderly in the
village where I grew up. My happy time was three
years ago when I went back and met up with my best
friend. It was something very special. I'm old now,
but I would like to visit again.'

MAVIS

85 years old

'You have to go through some terrible things in this
world to live you know, it's like when we first came here,
we'd been through enough hell. But you know, these
Black people can stand a lot of disaster, we're made for
that kind of thing. You white people, you worse, they
can't take nothing at all.

Me is a happy person, it the best thing that I do.
You don't sit down and have any stress, that is one of
the big killer. You keep sorry for yourself and all
that, no, you die before time.'

Margaret

86 years old

'I can dance without my stick if someone's holding onto me.'

NOBBY

87 years old

'I worked from 15 to 74. I met Doreen at work.
Me mum always used to do me banana sandwiches,
so I had to give up my banana sandwiches when
I went to the canteen to see Doreen. I got her bread
and jam ones. Turns out we were born a week apart
in the same hospital.

We enjoy our retirement. We don't get up early,
we get up when we wake up. We stay up late watching
films and that. We don't plan in front. You know, at
our age, we say every day is a bonus.'

HYACINTH

88 years old

'I used to love dancing. I used to go to six dances in one night and then not get up till three on a Sunday. Then I reached an age where I say, this not for me. Take it easy.'

MAUREEN

89 years old

'My husband chose to die, he was sick of all his
treatment. When he first went on the machine he said
to me, "Maureen, if ever the day comes when I've had
enough of this and I say to you, will you let me go?"
And I said, "Yes, I will." So when it happened, when
he said he wanted to go, I let him. I respected what
he wanted.'

ROSE

90 years old

'My friend Dolly James was a real laugh. When we were
sitting in a pie and mash shop, people used to stop
and stand by the door and watch us. These posh people
had never seen a pie shop before. That did make us
giggle, being gawped at. I never really drank, but she
used to drink like a fish. I used to go round every
morning for a gossip. She's died now, she was my best
friend. I don't have a best friend now, not like that,
I do miss her. We always used to have a laugh together.'

KATE

91 years old

'I miss going to work, I do, because it made you get
up, it made you have a wash, make yourself look nice,
a bit of make-up, ship out to work, talk to the girls.
Here – sometimes I don't get up till bleedin' 11 o'clock.
What's that all about?'

Irene

92 years old

'I did an abseil when I was 91 to raise money for the
St. Joseph's Hospice. I want to do the cheese cutter,
52 flights up. I'm going through my bucket list. I've
done a paraglide, two parachute jumps. I want to swim
with sharks, but it's a bit blimmin' cold at the moment.'

RON

93 years old

'My mother had me at 15, she was a Russian prostitute.
I'm not against that because she did it to keep alive.
My father was a Chinese Mafia man, he showed her
how to set up an opium den on Shacklewell Lane.
If a man came into the flat he was an "uncle". I had
so many different uncles.

I was moved between guardians. I was beaten but
in those days you couldn't really complain. I was what
you call an urchin. I ended up in reform school but
when the war came in 1939 I was released. I was 14.

There's such a lot to say when you're my age – you'd
better stop me if I go on. I was down the coal mines,
and I was in the army, I was a blocks man on a
fishmonger's stall, I worked on a bacon stove, had
a stall selling shirts down the market, I was an artist.

The greatest thing about me? I've been a professional
flamenco dancer most of my life.'

June

94 years old

'I was set up on two blind dates on the same day. One was with the man who became my husband, and the other was Eric Morecambe. I turned down Eric.'

ANNIE

95 years old

'It's only recently that my legs got bad. Oh, it is a
nuisance. Only last year I was doing the conga. I had
the policeman's hat on. Always the first to get up
and have a dance. I've always liked a good party.

I do try to do things. Now and again I get up a ladder
still. Last week I put my curtains up meself to save
my son a job. I gave it a wiggle before I climbed up.
I was alright. He did tell me off when he got here and
saw I'd put them up.'

IRENE

96 years old

'He was such a nice person, my husband, not one of
these flashy types. The thing we was ever choked about,
was that we couldn't have children. He said to me at
the time, when we come from the hospital – he could
see I was upset and he just got hold of me – and he said,
"Never mind, we're together."'

TED

97 years old

'If you get a good partner, you've got it, to my
mind. If you have your arguments, just go with
it. At the end of the day these little rucks don't
matter. Share your journey with someone.'

REBECCA

98 years old

'I had my birthday in Antigua. When I was on
the plane they gave me a bottle of champagne.
All the family, the children, the grandchildren
and the great-grandchildren, they were all there
on the beach to celebrate with me.'

ALEC

99 years old

'I don't feel any different to when I was 30 or 40.
Or 20, to be honest. When my daughter was round a
few years ago, I was using a pickaxe in the garden and
she started taking photos. I couldn't understand why.
She said, "Dad, not many people use a pickaxe when
they are 95."'

RENEE

100 years old

'I've got a past alright. I married a gangster, he thought
he was Humphrey Bogart, used to wear a white mac.
I was 21 at the time, in too deep to get out.

He went to prison for ten years the day after my son
was born. Sometimes I'd fold up a £20 note in my
mouth, and when I visited him I'd kiss him and pass
it to him in his mouth.

My boyfriend now is 28 years younger than me.
I became frail six or seven years ago and Terry said to
me, "I will never leave you. I'll always make sure
you're alright." We've never lived together, but every
night he rings and says I love you.'

ACKNOWLEDGEMENTS

Special thanks to Sophie Howarth who passed this idea to Hoxton Mini Press, suggesting it would be in safe hands with me; it has been a wonderful gift.

To the people of east London who are the subjects, cheerleaders and casting directors of this project, introducing me to their neighbours and grandparents: you are the best. I can't name you all in case I miss someone, but I know you'll look through and find your contributions.

Thank you to Kaoru and Graeme at Touch Digital for working on the files so patiently via Zoom when Covid meant we couldn't sit together. To Alona Pardo with her keen eye along the way, and Tracy Marshall for her belief in the project. The Photobook Club: my photo family with their insight and advice. To Claire and Debbie who generously helped with transcribing when I was overwhelmed and for encouraging me to keep going when I questioned continuing the work.

To Philip Glanville, the Mayor of Hackney, for his support, tweeting the ages I was struggling to find, and Jim Boddington GP who led me to the elder subjects who were hidden from view during 2020.

To my kids, Ruby and Herb, for their honest and opinionated views, never tiring of discussing every face, every story. And of course Duncan, who has supported and encouraged me through another long and obsessive project that stole many family hours.

It's been a treat to work with Lucy Davies again, thank you for the poetic introduction to this book and working through hours of interviews to offer up nuggets of magic to share. Thank you also to the Hoxton Mini Press team who have taken another punt on me and given this project a lot of considered time and patience. And to David Sedaris, who made some insightful, if brutal, edit suggestions for the text.

It's taken a whole community to bring this book together, it would have been an impossible task without you all.

Jenny Lewis, 2021